Stock Trading

Investing for Beginners 1 and The Predictable Stock Trading System

By Sam Sutton and Stephen Smith

Investing for Beginners

Simple Investing Guide to Become an Intelligent Investor

By Sam Sutton

Table of Contents

Introduction 6

Chapter 1: Why You Should Be Growing Your Money.................8

Chapter 2: How Compound Interest Works...........................11

Chapter 3: Things to Know Before You Invest 16

Chapter 4: Investing in Stocks..23

Chapter 5: Investing in Real Estate...................................27

Chapter 6: Investing in Bonds...32

Chapter 7: Investing in Business Partnerships 34

Chapter 8: Investing in Precious Metals..............................37

Chapter 9: Investing Strategies 39

Conclusion...43

The Predictable Stock Trading System

Introduction 49

Chapter 1 Basics for Beginners 51

Chapter 2 Let's Talk About Capital..................................53

Chapter 3 How to Use Money 60

Chapter 4 What Trading is NOT.......................................63

Chapter 5 Social Trading..71

Chapter 6 Trading and Time...73

Chapter 7 Trading and Commitment 77

Chapter 8 Compound Interest 80

Chapter 9 Investing in Yourself......................................82

Chapter 10 Should You Challenge the Market?.....................83

Chapter 11 Portfolios and Diversification............................84

Conclusion..86

Description 87

assurance regarding its continued validity or interim quality. Trademarks that mentioned are done without written consent and can in no way be considered an endorsement from the trademark holder.

Introduction

Thank you for your purchase of *Investing for Beginners*.

The following chapters will discuss everything you need to know to become an expert in the world of investing. Investing your hard-earned money in the most prosperous places may seem daunting, but it doesn't have to be! With this simple and easy-to-learn guide, you can learn the ins and outs of investing in a variety of markets in no time!

With this book, you will be able to build a strong foundation that will lead you to feel confident in where and who you are investing all that green in! Don't just wing it, but genuinely learn it.

You will acquire all the knowledge you need to get yourself started in the realm of successful investing. Who knows, perhaps you are worth hundreds of thousands *or more*, and you just don't know it yet!

Thanks again for choosing *Investing for Beginners*. Every effort was made to ensure it is full of as much useful information as possible, please enjoy!

Did you know that a large percent of people who make a lot of money lose it within the first couple years?

It doesn't take much for a person to lose all of their money. Around 2 in 3 lottery winners lose all of their winnings within 5 years. If someone could lose hundreds of millions of dollars over a couple years, how fast will you lose your millions that you could make from this book?

Over the past couple years I have stumbled upon the key secret behind managing money and KEEPING it. If you follow the link below you will uncover the truth behind managing and keeping the money you make

>>> Click/Tap here to Learn the Secret Behind Money Management <<<

Chapter 1: Why You Should Be Growing Your Money

You know what they say, "you have to have money to make money!" The same is totally true when it comes to investing. Endowing your hard-earned dollars gives you the power to put that money on a path to earning strong rates of return. If you don't invest, you are essentially missing out on awesome opportunities to increase your worth financially. While there is a chance to lose money when you invest, if you do so wisely, the potential gain is much more rewarding than the loss of never taking the action to invest.

These are the best reasons to invest your money starting now:

Cultivate Your Money

Obviously, the act of investing your money places it in a vehicle such as bonds, stocks, certificates of deposit, etc. These offer a return on the money you put aside to invest over a long period of time. These sorts of returns allow you to build your money, which helps it to grow to increase your financial wealth over time.

Build Your Retirement

When we are young and start working to make ends meet in the adult world, many of us do not even think about putting money aside for retirement. Many are unaware of their tolerance for risk, which inhibits people from considering putting money into investment avenues. The reality is, the greater the risk comes a better chance of earning a greater amount of wealth. The best places to invest your money when you are younger is in precious metals, businesses, real estate, mutual funds, bonds, and stocks.

Your mindset when it comes to investing should change over time, however. You need to become more conservative as you age, especially as you reach the age of retirement. You don't want to lose all that money you worked so hard to invest!

Acquire Higher Returns

If you desire to watch your money grow, you will need to invest it in places that have a high rate of return. You will earn more money the higher this return is. Many avenues of investment offer opportunities for you to earn high rates of returns. So, if you wish to earn a higher rate, you will need to do some exploring before investing your money.

Reach Your Financial Goals

Investing is a great method of reaching your large financial aspirations. When your money is earning a higher rate of interest, you are earning much more over time than you would by simply placing money in a savings account. The return on your investments can be used later in life to be put towards financial goals, such as buying a car, putting a down-payment on a home, starting a business, or getting your children through college.

Build on Pre-Tax Dollars

Some avenues of investing, such as employer-sponsored 401(k)s, let you invest your pre-taxed dollars. Having this option gives you the opportunity to save more money than just investing your post-taxed income.

Qualify for Employer-Matching Programs

There are a few employers out there that will offer their employees the chance to match the money you invest within your 401(k) up to a planned amount. The only way you can qualify for this opportunity is if you invest in your 401(k). This is the main reason many decide to invest in their company's 401(k) plans so they can gain the matching employer funds.

Begin and Build Businesses

Investing is a vital aspect of starting a business and expanding it. It also plays a role in helping other businesses expand. Many investors enjoy supporting entrepreneurs and devoting to the creation of new products and potential jobs. Investors truly love the part of their jobs where they can be part of the process in establishing contemporary businesses and assisting in building them to be successful that an, in turn, create a strong return on their investment.

Opportunity to Support Others

Investors sincerely like investing in other people, no matter if they are manufacturers, artists, business owners, etc. They feel good about helping other people achieve their goals.

Reduce Your Taxable Income

Being an investor allows you to reduce your overall taxable income by the act of investing pre-tax dollars into a retirement fund. When you generate from an investment loss, you can apply those losses against the gains you receive from other investments, which results in a decrease in the amount of taxable income.

Be a Part of a Brand-New Venture

New ventures are always in need of a backing of money. People starting new businesses look for investors to back them up. Investors like the thrill of being a part of creating something cutting-edge and being a part of something that introduces them to a whole new world.

Chapter 2: How Compound Interest Works

By putting your money in a credit union or bank, you are paid a certain amount of interest for being patient and letting your money sit in their financial institution. You must change your mindset towards interest and view it as a great thing. When you take the action of putting money into an investment account, the interest made is working for *you*.

What is Compound Interest?

The act of compounding simply means that you are gaining interest on the interest that has already accumulated on an investment you made. It is the act of exponential increase of your investment. Compounding functions as a process of creating a return on an asset's reinvested earnings. It requires two vital pieces to work properly:

1. The reinvestment of earning
2. Time

View compound interest as a personal assistant that is able to help grow the investment you initially made. For those that are younger when they begin investing, compounding is by far the best tool, which is why it is highly recommended to start as early as you possibly can!

The Difference Between Compound Interest and Simple Interest

- **Simple interest** is received only from the earning of principal. For example, you have $1,000 that you were earning simple interest on at 2 percent each year, you would have made $20 a year on that $1,000. Your interest for the first year would be $20, as would the second, third, fourth, and so on years. The amount you earned would not change. By the time 40 years rolls around, you will have made around $1,800.

- **Compound interest** enables one to gain more interest on the interest they are earning from an investment. For example, if you have $1,000 and earn 2 percent each year following the initial investment with compounding interest, the outcome is

11

totally different than with simple interest. By the time you hit the end of your first year, you would have $1,020. By year two, you would end up with $20.40 instead of just $20. If you leave it alone for all 40 years, you will then have earned $2,200.00. That's more than $400 than utilizing the process of simple interest.

Creating Savings Over Time

As you can see, if you were to invest $1,000 in an account that only yielded 2 percent, your money would not grow at a very fast rate. The key to investing is constantly contributing money to that investment, which enables you with additional money that earns compound interest. The magical aspect of compound interest is that the more you contribute, the quicker you will see your money grow! Keep in mind that compound interest works better for you if you leave that money alone for a longer period of time. Again, a perfect reason to start early and build over time.

For example, let's say you are 25-years-old and you begin by investing $5,000 in a savings account. If you put $200 in each month during a span of 40 years, your money can grow as much as $158,900.00 by the time you reach the ripe old age of 65. If you contribute $500 each month for 40 years, you will have earned $380,700. But if you manage to start just five years later, you will only end up with $315,9oo+. See how starting early gives you the advantage of earning tens of thousands of more dollars?

Inflation

Another key aspect in the investment world is inflation, which has the potential to damage your potential for return. A good rule to follow when it comes to savings is to figure that inflation will be 3 to 4 percent each year. What this means for you is that you real returns will become eroded if your account fails to have a high yield. It is recommended to look for a savings product that offers higher yields in the first place, such as CDs, online savings account, etc.

Inflation may not be fighting against your yields at this very moment, but in the future, the rate of interest will likely rise. If you contribute more to your savings, you will find that your contributions will grow at a much quicker rate.

You Want to Earn Interest, Not Pay It

Compound interest is a pretty nifty tool, right? Beware, however, for it can function the opposite way as well.

Let's take a credit card company for example. A typical one charges around 20% in interest on unpaid balances each month. If you have an unpaid balance of $1,000, it will turn to $1,200 of debt by the time the year ends. You need to reverse the load of debt you have by applying the principles of compound interest. Transfer credit card debt to an interest plan with lower rates. Or, pick a loan with a yearly interest payment, instead of one with a monthly or quarterly required payment.

There are many investment vessels you can use to build up your compounding as well as maximize your efforts to build wealth:

High-Interest Savings Accounts

These accounts can be hard to come by, but by doing a bit of digging, you can find some awesome rates. If you are wanting to invest now, you should seek out banks that update their interest rates on a regular basis. Just a few percentage points can make a world of difference.

For instance, if you invest $5,000 in an account that grows 0.8 percent of compound interest within a period of 5 years, your return will be $5,200. But the same investment of $5,000 at a rate of 2 percent will yield you $5,500. For that extra $300, it is worth that extra time to locate a better interest rate to invest your money into. Bankaholic is a great start for consumers in the United States, and High-Interest Savings is a good choice for Canadian consumers.

Another good thing that brings you peace of mind is that the going rates on bank websites are often negotiable. Before you agree to a set rate, no matter if it is for a car payment, savings account, or load, ask the provider if they have any discretion. You might get an interesting look, but just for asking, the lender may just provide you the best rate available!

Certificate of Deposit (CDs)

CD's are very secure vehicles of investment, for they offer a fixed rate of interest till they hit a specific date of maturity. The advantage of CDs over high-interest savings accounts is that they guarantee that the interest rate will not change during the time you are investing. The catch is, your money is not liquid, which means you have to keep it locked away for a specific period of time. If you go to withdrawal it early than that date, you will have to pay a penalty. What you earn from the interest is also taxable.

There are various kinds of CDs and GICs (Guaranteed Investment Certificates). Each has their own set of terms, as well as pros and cons. As of now, CD and GIC rates of interest are about even with accounts that have high interest rates.

Stock Dividend Payments

Stocks that pay you dividends are a fantastic way to add additional income to your life. To grasp the absolute power of investing in these kinds of payments, read this example of the story of Grace Groner:

Grace was hired as a secretary after she graduated college in 1931. She worked for 40 years in this position. Grace did not earn an amazing salary as a secretary. She bought clothes from thrift stores and personal home sales and lived in a tiny apartment that was given to her after a friend died.

A few years later in 1935, Grace purchased a few shares of the company's stock that she worked for, at $60 per share. Her investment total was $200. Grace did not sell her share. Through the ways of share splits, dividends, and dividend reinvesting, when she passed away in 2010, her portion of the shares was worth over $7 million. By simply starting with $200, Grace was able to take full advantage of the power of compounding for roughly 75 years.

The Answer to Investing

By grasping how to maximize the usage of compounding interest, you too can harbor the power to create a substantial chunk of wealth over time. The vital key to keep in mind is that no matter how good or bad your finances are right now, you can change your financial future thanks to compounding.

Chapter 3: Things to Know Before You Invest

Many people never take the time to invest because they follow their belief of "my money is not safe within the markets." This is the conclusion many folks have, especially after the devastation the markets faced back in 2008. Stocks were sold, and many watched their 401k's become 201 and even 101k's. But now, those who had little faith in the markets before are started to get their feet wet in the world of investing once again. The stock market has since been doing spectacularly and proving all those skeptical journalists dead wrong.

Are you considering getting back into investing in the market? Well now might be the most perfect time to avoid the errors that many trap investors use to eat away at their gains. This chapter outlines how to invest your hard-earned money wisely with these valuable tips!

Know the Investing Costs

One of the biggest mistakes investors make is paying large amounts to invest their money. Stockbrokers, tax consultants, and financial advisors are not cheap and can easily eat away at any gains you receive within your investment portfolio.

The fees that Wall Street hides from investors is in the tiny print on your quarterly statements. And even if you were to take the time to read them, you would probably have a very hard time even understanding what they say. If you fail to learn what fees you are being charged with, you probably should avoid those services in the first place. Rule of thumb: if the fees are not completely clear and easy to understand, avoid them at all costs.

Here are the biggest sources of costs it takes to invest that you should keep in mind:

- **Inflation** is an ultimate killer of investment portfolios. If your gains of investment fail to keep ahead of inflation, you will lose money because the value of your money gets eroded away.

- When your investment advisor informs you how much you have made, they are more than likely talking about your gains before **taxes**. But the reality is, you never actually take home your pre-tax gains, just the after-tax ones. You must understand how the tax system will take care of your investments. You will also need to keep in mind what future development of the tax codes might be and how they will affect your investments as well.

- Mutual funds and brokers will charge you a fraction of the amount based on how big or small your portfolio is, which are known as **advisory fees**. Often times the number they charge is so small that you do not think much about it, but 2 percent can add up quicker than you think.

- Each time you sell or purchase a stock, a fee is charged by your brokerage, known as **brokerage commissions**. They are typically flat fees based upon either the amount of stock you buy or the trade. The lower, the better is the best way to go here.

Decrease Your Costs

Since you are now aware of the costs that can damage your overall portfolio, you are now in a place where you need to figure out methods of decreasing them. Here are the best things you can do to counteract those fees:

- **Invest in mutual and index funds that cost the lowest**. This obviously seems pretty straightforward, but many investors overlook this simplicity. There are very small fractions of a percent that can make a huge impact on your portfolio over many years.

- **Pay attention to cost changes.** Even though you invested in a low-cost fund, to begin with, does not mean that the costs will stay low. New competitors and products are introduced to the world all the time, which may play a role in increasing your fees.

- **Pay Capital Gains, not Income Taxes.** Active brokerage accounts or investment funds that generate many sales will also create high taxes on gains. You can reduce your tax costs by sticking funds that are passive and can make investments long-term. You will pay lower capital instead of those high-income taxes. Just be aware that some eliminated this benefit to investors.

- **Purchase Inflation Protected Treasuries.** To decrease becoming exposed to the inflation process, you can purchase gold, which has a tendency to go up in value when the value of money decreases. But this is not a practical method for the majority of investors. A simpler method is to put part of your overall portfolio in a TIPS, or a Treasury Inflation Protected Securities. While this will not shield you from collapses in the government, it can protect you from about everything else.

- **Invest in a Retirement Account.** If you are investing to mainly save up for retirement, ensure that you are utilizing an account that is also paired with tax advantages that let you avoid taxes not only now but in the future as well. This advantage can take you far, and the good news is that many big employers offer these accounts.

Gain Exposure to Upside Surprises

As an investor, you will get a first-hand look at how unpredictable the market is. This is a big problem for many investors because you are only allowed to invest for the gains you hope you will have in the future. As an investor, you are also a speculator for uncertainty in future events.

One way to handle all that uncertainty is to create a situation of upside exposure. What this means is that you should be willing to put money down on a number like you do when playing roulette. In other words, do not be stupid and make big bets randomly. Search and locate events that look highly unlikely, something that many others say is unlikely to occur. Make a small investment in that event, just remember that the odds are stacked against you.

For example, buying a $1 lottery ticket is not a good way to expose yourself to the upside of winning. This is because your investment of that dollar is too much for many jackpots in the first place. But if you purchase a lottery ticket with just a few coins of change, that would make more sense. The point here is, making riskier bets is perfectly fine as long as the cost to make them is low.

Diversify

Everyone has learned not to put all your "eggs in one basket." Diversifying your investments is vital. But many do not grasp how challenging it is to really diversify their money. Here are some pointers to get started:

- **Have more than one manager.** Many people think they are diversified because of the assortment of assets they had listed in their portfolios. The sad truth is many investors are exposed to a whole different type of risk, which is getting ripped off by their asset manager. Diversification should happen in every level.

- **Time preference.** Your investment portfolio should have assets in it that you expect to appreciate at different increments of time. This is a heavily overseen aspect of investing. Doing this helps you to avoid having those investments to be keyed in all at once, possibly during a time when the market could very well be crashing.

- **Mix assets.** You are not diversified if you own twenty or even one-hundred stocks and not anything else. You should strive to have a variety of classes when it comes to assets, such as treasuries, gold, bonds, stocks, etc. This makes you *truly* diversified.

Engage in Legal Insider Trading

If you hold a piece of valuable intel about an organization that you know others do not have access to, you should think about trading on that intel. There is nothing illegal about trading information that is secret that took you lots of hard work to come across. This is one of the best and only ways you can ever beat the market.

Here is the catch, however; do not do this if the intel that you withhold about an organization is one that you or a spouse works for. Do not act on this even if you hold an obligation to a third party. You can easily violate SEC rules when trading non-public information from a place of business you work for.

Don't Fall for "Hot Stocks"

Every single year some businesses run features in papers and magazines about hot stocks and sectors that are coming up. Honestly, you should never read these articles and avoid them as much as possible. The only thing these do is cause you distraction.

The same concept is true for investing in advice from people like Mr. Jim Cramer. When markets open the following morning, a stock that Cramer recommended is more than likely way to pricey. If you really want to place money in these hot stocks, wait a couple to a few months. If it goes down and you still think it is a good investment for your money, go for it. But the key here is to avoid that initial rush of wanting to trade by going for the bait of when it is first announced.

Ignore Most of Your Quarterly Statement (But Still Read it!)

Let's be honest, who really *likes* to read their statements in the first place? This is especially true when the market is not ideal. They will make you feel poor, ignorant, and can bring down your overall self-esteem when it comes to investing. But yes, you need to *read your statement!* You should not be reading them for your returns, but rather to keep track of those investing fees. Many brokerages and funds tap on extra fees in hopes that investors will not notice them.

Negotiation is Possible for Just About Anything

If you are signing on to investing in a sizeable fund, expect to pay the required fees. If you plan to create a brokerage account, however, you have a lot more room to negotiate what these fees are.

Financial advisors will say the fees are set at a certain rate and cannot be changed, but do not believe them. There is a plethora of fees offered by brokerages. The thing is, they are not obligated to find the best-priced ones for you. You need to negotiate with your broker to find the lowest fee they can. Once they give you a quote, simply tell them "these are not the fees I am looking for."

Invest in Passive Life Cycle Funds and Reinvest with Dividends

This tip can be a daunting one that takes some work, but welcome to the world of investing! The best thing you can do to set yourself up for success in the realm of investment is to invest your money in a lifecycle fund that is low in cost. These funds can change your allocation of assets as your age.

You should also take the step of reinvesting those dividends in your funds. Each year you should take the time to examine fees and every five years ask for assistance in analyzing your asset allocation. If you get divorced, buy a house, get married, have children, etc., you will want to re-examine these allocations.

You Will Never Be Able to Beat the Market

And you will not want to anyways! Here are crucial things you need to know when it comes to investing:

- Even if you were to learn how to beat the market, you could not beat it. If you try, you will more than likely end up farther behind than when you started.
- That being said, there really is no reason you should want to outsmart the market anyways. The great news here is that you

do not have to fight against the market to receive gains from your investments. The real goal of investing is to save money for later in life and not let it lose value. Investing is not about getting rich quickly.

- Sometimes, returns will be a lot worse then you expect them to be. In the future, diversified investment strategies might not pay off as well. Changes in demographics, the spread of information, the age of the average investor, and declining markets have huge impacts. Never count on bonds and stocks to go up along a trend for forever.

Chapter 4: Investing in Stocks

Let me ask you this: Would you rather have $108,000 or $600,000?

The answer for everyone is obviously the same! But how in the world can you as one person make $600,000?!

Well, start with investing $300, then add $300 monthly over the course of 30 years, and you will accumulate $108,000. But here is the difference when it comes to compounding at different interest rates:

- 2 percent = $147,600
- 5 percent = $245,600
- 10 percent = $620,700

The vital lesson to learn here is that saving is important, but what you *earn* on that saving is crucial to making more money with those investments. Sadly, in today's world, there is no method to earn anything close to that 10 percent when it comes to insured savings accounts. It is even challenging to earn 2 percent at times. The only method to get a higher rate of return is to take a risk and invest in stocks.

What Are Stocks?

Stocks are equity investments that serve as a part of ownership within a business. They entitle you to a part of that corporations earning and assets. **Common stocks** provide shareholders voting right, but no actual guarantee that they will receive dividend payments. The **preferred stocks** offer no right to vote but promise those dividend payments.

Shareholders receive a paper certificate of their stock, which is known as a security. This verifies the number of shares they own. But today, ownership is recorded electronically. This means that shares are held by your brokerage firm for safe keeping.

Stock investing can be awfully tricky. When it comes to successfully stock investing, you will need to get into a business mindset. Before you go out and purchase a stock, you should master all of the fundamental parts that make up investing. You will not become an investor overnight, but once you grasp the basics, you only then should be investing in stocks. This way, you have the confidence to make the right decisions.

Depending on how you measure stocks, they have averaged around 8 to 10 percent annually over the past century. Stocks always involve risk, which is why they pay much more than the average saving account. If you avoid risk, you create a whole new risk, which is not having enough money to adequately survive in your years of well-deserved retirement.

Stock knowledge is important! And contrary to popular belief, it is not rocket science.

The Rules of Investing in Stocks

Rule #1: Only Long-Term Money

Stocks would not even exist if they did not pay more than the alternatives that are less risky. The key phrase in this rule to remember is "over time." The longer your investment, the lower the risk when it comes to stocks.

Day trading is strongly risky because no one really knows what is going to occur each day. If you are not one to be extremely risky with their money, aim to invest in quality stocks because they show more value over time historically.

Rule #2: Moderation

Since the stock market is risky, it is vital to never put all your money in one place. If you are 25-years-old, for example, you should subtract your age from 100. This means that 75 percent should be put into stocks and the other 25 percent should be placed in savings.

Rule #3: Utilize Mutual Funds

Many people like purchasing individual stocks, but it is not necessary. You can function perfectly fine with a mutual fund as you lower your risk of reducing hassle at the same time.

Mutual funds are essentially a big pool of investments. It can be both a stock pool, which is a pool of stocks or a bond pool, a pool of bonds. Or, some mutual funds withhold both stocks and bonds, which is called a balanced fund.

Mutual funds allow you to spread the risk of investing in stocks by diversification among many stocks instead of just in a few. They also have people in them that do both the buying and selling and they keep track of the majority of that pesky paperwork for you.

Mutual funds fall into two categories:

- **Index funds** is similar to owning the entire stock market but is represented with an index. All the index fund managers have to do is buy the stocks, making it simple, and the fees minimal.
- **Actively managed funds** employ folks that claim they can outperform the indexes in index funds. They demand higher fees for their expertise.

Rule #4: Do Not Time the Market

You will quickly find yourself sitting on the sidelines if you try to time the market, especially when and if it takes off or crashes. There is a simple way to approach the stock market: with dollar cost averaging, which is also referred to as systematic investing. To do this, all you must do is invest in fixed amounts, such as $100 during regular intervals. This method works well because it automatically purchases more shares when they are cheaper, and fewer shares when they are more expensive.

Rule #5: There Are No Rules!

If you do not plan to take a bit of a risk, you will never reap the rewards. The trick to lessen the nightmares of investing is to be wise about it. No rule states you must invest in stocks. If you dislike stocks, invest elsewhere, such as collectibles, peer-to-peer lending, side businesses, real estate, etc. There are many other avenues to beat the bank. While some involve more time and risk than others, their rewards can have the potential to change your life.

Chapter 5: Investing in Real Estate

Purchasing real estate is a lot more than locating a new place to call a home of your own. Investing in real estate has been over time a progressive way to invest hard-earned cash and is a very prevalent investment vehicle.

The real estate market has tons of room to pocket huge gains by purchasing and owning. It is significantly more complicated than just placing investments into stocks and bonds.

Rental Properties

This is a venture that is as aged as the practice of owning land. People will purchase a property and lease it out to an inhabitant. The proprietor, known as the owner of the land, is then in charge of paying the loan, assessments, and expenses of keeping up with the property.

The proprietor charges lease to cover the greater part of the costs. A landowner may charge more since their goal to make a profit. However, the most widely used method is persistence, so they just charge enough lease to cover costs until the home loan has been paid in full, then the lease moves toward becoming a solid investment. The property may have appreciated in value through the time the loan was active, leaving the proprietor with a profitable resource.

There are, obviously, flaws in this seemingly "perfect venture." You can end up with a terrible occupant who destroys the property or you will end up having no inhabitant at all. This then leaves you with a negative income, leaving you to scramble to cover your home loan installments. This is why you should always opt for a territory where opening rates are low and pick a place that individuals will have to lease.

When you purchase a stock, it sits in your fund and over time, creates increments in value. When you invest in rental properties, many obligations come with being a proprietor. If the heater quits working, it's you who gets the telephone call. If you do not mind being a part-time and unpaid handyman, this may not bother you in the slightest. If you have the money and are willing to pay for these issues to be taken off your hands, it is a good investment to hire a property supervisor who would be more than happy to assist.

Real Estate Investment Groups

Real estate investment groups are similar to small shared assets for investment properties. If you wish to own a property to rent out, but do not wish to deal with all the hassles that being a landlord has to offer, a real estate investment group is more than likely a much better option.

An organization will buy or create a group of apartments or condos which then enable speculators to get them through the organization, they then allow them to join this group. A financial specialist can then claim one or various units of living space, but the people working the investment manage all of the units, which include dealing with upkeep, promoting empty units and meeting occupants. In return for this kind of management, the organization takes a percentage of the lease.

There are a few variants of investment groups, yet in a regular form, the rent is in the financial specialist's name and the units get together a bit of all the lease agreements to prepare for infrequent opening, implying that you will get enough to pay the home loan regardless of whether your unit is never actually leased out.

The nature of investment groups depends on the organization that is offering it. It is a protected method to get into real estate investment, yet many are still defenseless against expenses that frequent the mutual fund industry. Once again, performing adequate research is key to success.

Real Estate Trading

This is the intriguing and challenging side of real estate investing. Like investors who are miles away from a purchase, the land brokers are an altogether unique group. Land brokers buy properties with a goal to have them for a brief time, around three to four months. This is when they plan to offer their property purchase for an investment. This procedure is called flipping properties and is focused on purchasing properties that are either underestimated or are in an exceptionally hot market.

Unadulterated property flippers won't put any cash into a house for upgrades; the investment needs to have the incentive to turn a profit without adjustment or they will pass it by. If a property flipper gets captured in a circumstance where he or she can't empty a property, it can be damaging to the financial specialists as it would mean don't keep enough prepared money to pay the home loan on a property. This can prompt misfortunes for a land broker who can't offload the property in a terrible market.

An inferior of property flipper likewise exists. These financial specialists profit by purchasing sensibly evaluated properties and including an incentive by remodeling them. This can be a more drawn out term which relies on upgrades. The restricting part of this journey is that it takes time and just enables financial specialists to go up against one property at any given moment.

REITs

Real estate has been around since practically the dawn of time, where our ancestors who were cave dwellers began to chase out strangers from their space. It is no wonder that Wall Street has figured out how to turn real estate into a trade on an open market.

A real estate investment trust (REIT) is created when a trust, also known as an organization, utilizes a financial specialists' money to purchase and work salary properties. REITs are bought and sold on significant trades, much the same as some other stock. To keep up the status as a REIT, an organization must give out 90% of its benefits as profits. REITs are then abstained from paying corporate income tax, though a standard organization would be saddled by its benefits. After that need to choose if they wish to circulate its after-impose benefits as profits.

Much like standard profit paying stocks, REITs are a strong venture for securities exchange financial specialists that need customary wage. In contrast with the previously mentioned kinds of land speculation, REITs permit speculators into non-private ventures, for example, shopping centers or office structures and are exceedingly fluid. At the end of the day, you won't require a real estate broker to enable you to money out your venture.

Leverage

Except for REITs, putting resources into real estate provides a financial specialist a device that isn't accessible to securities speculators, which is the use of the REIT. If you are looking to buy a stock, you need to pay the entire estimation of the stock at the time your request. Regardless of whether you are purchasing on the boundary, the sum you receive is still substantially less than with real estate.

Many "traditional" home loans require a 25 percent down-payment that is contingent upon where you reside. There is a plethora of types of home loans that require just a tiny 5 percent. This shows that you can control the entirety of the property and its value by paying a small amount of the aggregate esteem. Obviously, the loan will, in the long-term, pay the estimation of the house at the time you purchased it, but you are still in control of the moment the papers are agreed on.

This is an aspect that encourages both the flippers of real estate properties and owners of real estate. They can make a temporary contract on their homes and put up front installments on more than one property. Regardless of whether they lease these out with the goal that inhabitants pay the loan or they sit tight for a chance to receive a greater investment, they are in full control, in spite of having paid for just a piece of the aggregate esteem.

The Bottom Line

We have taken a gander at a few kinds of real estate investing methods. Nonetheless, we have just touched the most superficial layer. Inside these cases, there are endless varieties of ways to invest in real estate.

Likewise, with any venture, there are huge amounts of overall potential when it comes to real estate. This does not imply that it is a guaranteed gain. Make watchful decisions and weigh out all of the pros and cons of your activities before taking a dive into the real estate game.

Chapter 6: Investing in Bonds

While the word "bonds" sounds awfully boring, it is far from it. They are a safe haven for retired and rich folks that do not wish to lose their money. Bonds play a role in your investment plan for other reasons as well. They help add diversity to your portfolio as they control risk. However, bonds can be a complicated subject to thoroughly grasp.

Bonds are completely different from sticks. Stocks that are well-selected tend to go up over a long period of time but can go down in the short run. Bonds also create a very nice steady stream of income that you can then reinvest or utilize for living expenses later on. Their price has the potential to fluctuate, but the overall bond remains the same. Plus, bonds like municipal ones can produce a tax-free income!

Getting Started with Bonds

It is crucial to understand the concepts of price, interest, maturity, and yield before jumping into making an investment in a bond. Small investors should really stick with high-quality bonds.

- Interest: The majority of bonds pay you interest semiannually.
- Maturity: When a bond reaches its maturity, they then have the power to pay the investor back at face value. Bonds that mature in two years or less are short-term ones, with 10 years being intermediate and 10+ years being long-term bonds. Most bonds are issues with 20 to 30 years maturity.

Types of Bonds

- **Zero-Coupon Bonds:** Many common bonds you receive interest payments every six months. But with zero-coupon ones, they credit you interest. However, it doesn't pay till it totally matures.
- **Uncle Sam's Bonds:** If you like peace of mind, these types of bonds are the essential way to go!

- o **Treasury bills** mature in a year or less with new ones being sold on a weekly basis. The minimum amount to purchase is $1,000. They are exempt from local and state taxes as well.
- o **Treasury bonds** take 10 or more years to mature. The minimum to purchase one of these bonds is $1,000.
- **U.S. Agency Securities:** Are similar to government bonds when it comes to safety, but be aware of the risks they hold as well.
- **Municipal Bonds:** These depend on which bracket you are when it comes to taxes. The higher the tax bracket, the more likely you will receive a better benefit than those that are issued by local and state agencies.

Chapter 7: Investing in Business Partnerships

Investing your hard-earned cash into a business is one of the best and most prevalent methods of investing in the journey of financial dependence for those small businesses. It is a great way to grow and create an asset that, when led under proper conditions, provides numerous amounts of cash those other investments cannot compete with. Small businesses grow through the means of representing the most crucial financial resource the family owns, other than their home.

Investments in business are built as either a limited partnership or a limited liability company. The limited liability is by far the most used, for it combines the best attributes of corporation and partnerships. When you are pondering over investing your money into a small business, there are two main types of positions you can choose to take:

Equity Investments

When you make an equity investment in any business, you are essentially purchasing part of the overall ownership, or in other words, taking a piece of the pie. Equity investors give capital with cash in exchange for the percentage of both profits and losses.

The business then can utilize this allotment of money for a variety of things that are business related, from funding expenditures, the running of daily operations, decreasing debts, purchasing other owners, creating liquidity, or hiring new employees. This type of investment when it comes to small businesses results in bigger gains but comes with a bit more risk. If expenses become higher than the amount of sales, the losses get handed over to the investor. If things go well, the return can be exponential.

Debt Investments

When you make a debt investment in a business, you are loaning money in exchange for repayment of your loan down the road, along with income made from interest. Debt capital is given in the form of loads with amortization or the purchasing of bonds that are issued by the business itself.

The biggest advantage to debt investments is that you get a nice cozy spot in the structure of capitalization. This means that if the company fails, the debt takes priority over stockholders, also known as equity investors. The highest level of debt incurred is a first mortgage secured loan that has a lien on a piece of property or an asset that is very valuable, typically the brand name.

Which Type of Partnership Investment is Better?

When it comes to life in general, especially when it comes to the subject of businesses, there is no simple or clean-cut answer. For example, if you were an early investor of McDonald's and purchased equity, you would be very well off. If you had purchased bonds with the debt investment method, you would have earned a decent amount in return, but by no means as spectacular as the other.

Things to Know Before Investing in Partnerships

- **Beware of the opportunity** by asking why the opportunity is available for investing in the first place. Usually, businesses are trying to raise money, which usually means they failed to get a loan from a bank. You need to find out the story behind their reasonings.

- **Understanding the structure** can help you to determine how the legal systems and the IRS view the profits and liabilities of the business you are considering investing in. There are major chances that the business could fall out. You can be responsible for bills that are unpaid or other liabilities depending on the structure of the business.

- **Keep in mind that you may not see returns for years**, so do not assume that investing in a business will equal automatic profit. Startups especially need all the money they can get, with earnings usually being added back into the business. Returns for investors may not be present for 3 to 5 years or more.

- **Have an exit strategy planned** just in case it takes too long for you to see solid revenue from your investment. You do not want to burn through all your investment before a business opens its doors.

- **Do your homework** before investing your money into a startup business. You want to know the background of the business and have a good understanding of it and its competition. You should also request a business plan that includes a description, financial plan, market analysis, etc.

Chapter 8: Investing in Precious Metals

Investing in gold and silver is quite simple, as well as fun and highly profitable. Almost anyone can learn how to begin purchasing gold and silver as a physical way to wealth. Gold and silver, along with other precious metals, have the strength to hold their value, which can mean not only a beautiful but a long-term investment as well.

The process of purchasing, selling, and holding precious metals involves some annoyance that you need to understand to be successful and gain awesome returns.

What Are Precious Metals

Precious metals are naturally occurring, rare, and challenging to find than other metal types. The rarity of these metals gives them high economic value. They are still valued for their use in commodities, jewelry, art, and investments.

- Gold
- Silver
- Palladium
- Platinum

Precious Metal Investing

Precious metals are highly valued in many industries, so they are traded on a regular basis in world commodity markets. People in all countries have some sort of need for precious metals, which means they are constantly changing due to the supply and demand for them.

These metals can be bought by people as investment vehicles. This is done through a mint or a broker, in which it can be purchased in a few formats, such as in its physical form, stocks, mutual funds, ETF funds, etc. Those that choose to buy precious metals in their physical form usually purchase bars, bullion, or coins in various shapes and sizes, depending on the amount they purchased.

Inflation is a common risk when it comes to investing in metals. Buying them at the present time at the current price protects their value against future metal inflation, which is why they make for ideal investment vessels. This is certainly true with gold, the most popular investment metal due to its high value and availability.

Buying Precious Metals

Investing in precious metals is a great method if you are looking to make quick profits and increase your savings for future living. You can purchase or sell small to large amounts of metals on a regular basis to make money daily. You can also buy small to medium allotments to hold as a part of a retirement account.

The best metals to buy are silver and gold because they are the ones most often used as currency. You will need to talk to a stockbroker or a dealer of precious metals to buy them. You also will need to do adequate research on the various methods of precious metal investing to discover all the methods in which you can gain a profit from each precious metal individually and together.

Chapter 9: Investing Strategies

When it comes to investing, any amount of knowledge adds significant value to you as a growing investor in the market. This chapter is loaded with strategies to help you invest the best you can as a beginner in the world of investing.

Don't Wait, Start Now

There will never be a better time to begin the investing process. Don't wait till you get a higher paying job or save enough money. If you are a procrastinator, this will never come for you. Start now, with a little from each paycheck you receive. The quicker you start, the better you will be and the bigger of an investment you will incur over time as it matures.

Expert Advice

Experts in the investing world can help you to understand all of the investment options that are open to you. You will be able to determine which avenues of investing are right for your lifestyle with the help of an investment planner. Many are free! Open an account and link your accounts.

Start Out Simple

After you are knowledgeable about the options you have, it is recommended to start with the simplest and learn the rest as you gain experience. You can make mistakes and not feel bad about it when you are just starting out, with small investments like $100.

Know Your Goals

Before you make the step to invest, know what your goals are for venturing into investing in the first place. Do you want to start saving for retirement? Do you want to grow a fund for your kid(s) to go to college? Investing is much different from just saving money, it is a long-term process.

Know Your Options for Investment Vehicles

Make sure you plan out what you wish to invest in as well when deciding your goals. You can invest in brokerage accounts, college funds, 401k's, etc. Some of these have big tax breaks that will make them a clear advantage.

Open an Investment Account

Once you have made a clear decision about what vehicle you wish to use and what your goals are, it will be much easier to sign a form and get funds rolling into an account. Make sure you have a reliable platform to buy and sell your investments.

Start in Auto Investing

You should start this as soon as possible with regular contributions. Many brokerage accounts totally support monthly investment options.

Learn a Hands-On Approach

Many people think that once they make an investment, they just let it sit there and it will do the hard work for them. It is vital to track your investments to check to see if they are growing. Make it a priority to check into them every six months to a year.

Picking an Amount to Start Investing

This will be a major decision when it comes to handling your budgets and the increments you will make to your investment over time for it to grow substantially.

Make Investing a Habit

To increase your investment earnings over time, you have to stick to it and contribute regularly. It's kind of like a plant; if you don't water it and provide it with a light source, it will eventually die and not create any produce for you to pick.

Make Baby Steps

Don't expect investments you make to make anything extraordinary any time in the near future. You must learn to be patient and look into other investment options to invest money in as you wait for your others to grow over time.

Be Knowledgeable of Packaged Mutual Funds

This is a great option that many beginners in investing overlook. They are less risky and are quite volatile. The costs for transactions are also low, and every fund is easily managed by portfolio managers who are in charge of rebalancing your portfolio to ensure that proportions are consistent with your investment.

Be Wise When Choosing Stocks

You will never be able to accurately time a stock market, but they are a good option and don't require you to have a lot of capital upfront. If you pick wisely, you will have a peace of mind knowing you will have a stable income.

Take the Time to Learn

It is no secret that there is a lot of information regarding investing. If you are serious about becoming a seasoned investor, go out of your way to purchase investment books, strategize with the investment knowledge you gain. Look online and perform research, checking out companies that peak your interest. Ensure that you are fully aware of what those companies are earning, who their customers are, and more.

Play Safe

Investing is not the time of place to be wild with your money. Make a margin of safety for yourself, but be sure not to be too over-dramatic with your boundaries, as it could keep you from exploring other vehicles of investing or keeping you from taking the risks that are required in investing to reach success.

Don't Impulse Invest

Make sure to always take your time and speak with experts before going out and purchasing stocks, bonds, funds, or another other investment vehicle.

Beat Inflation

No matter what you choose to invest in, try your best to beat the rate of inflation, or you might find that you are losing money rather than gaining it. Simply placing your hard-earned money in a savings account is not a method of investment, but an easy-way-out of doing the hard work to reach your financial goals.

Create an Emergency Fund

Before you go out and start the process of building up your investment empire, make sure to create an emergency fund first. Also, it is a good idea to create an insurance cushion that will protect your money. You never know where the road to investment will lead you.

Conclusion

I want to congratulate you for making it to the end of *Investing for Beginners*!

I give you a big pat on the back for reading the entirety of this book, for you are one giant step closer to becoming your very own investor! While money can't buy happiness, it can sure help to build a cushion that brings you peace of mind when life gets a bit rocky. Wouldn't you rather be prepared than sorry?

As you have learned, everyone should learn the basics of investing. Now that you have soaked up all this valuable information, you should feel all that confidence bursting at the seams inside of you. Yes, you can even learn how to invest like the big guys on Wall Street with a bit of basic knowledge, common sense, and a bit of faith in the market.

I hope that everything in this book has given you the information you need to take the next step in investing some of that hard-earned money of yours. All the tools you need to achieve your investment goals can be found in this book as a reference if you get a bit lost.

Good luck my investing friends! Make that money grow!

If you found this book useful in any way, please take a moment from your investing ventures to leave a review on Amazon. It is always appreciated!

Did you know that a large percent of people who make a lot of money lose it within the first couple years?

Stock Trading

It doesn't take much for a person to lose all of their money. Around 2 in 3 lottery winners lose all of their winnings within 5 years. If someone could lose hundreds of millions of dollars over a couple years, how fast will you lose your millions that you could make from this book?

Over the past couple years I have stumbled upon the key secret behind managing money and KEEPING it. If you follow the link below you will uncover the truth behind managing and keeping the money you make

>>> Click/Tap here to Learn the Secret Behind Money Management <<<

Description

Looking to invest some of the money you have worked ages for but are not sure where to start? Congrats! You have come across just the right book!

No matter if you grew up in a family of wealthy investors or are just interested in learning the basics of what it takes, this book is for you! Everyone has to start somewhere, so why should you cause pain to yourself by attempting to read complicated jargon that makes absolutely no sense? No one has that much time to waste, and you certainly don't either!

Within this book, you will learn everything you need to know to build a strong foundation to learn the ins and out of the world of investing. Without this foundation, you are setting yourself up for failure and a loss of that hard-earned cash. No one deserves that! You deserve to know where you are putting your money and what places and strategies help it to grow more.

The Predictable Stock Trading System

Turn 1 Hour Of Stock Trading Per Day Into Generational Wealth

By Stephen Smith

As befitting its nature, it is presented without assurance regarding its prolonged validity or interim quality. Trademarks that are mentioned are done without written consent and can in no way be considered an endorsement from the trademark holder.

Introduction

Congratulations on downloading *Stock Trading* and thank you for doing so.

The following chapters will discuss what the stock market is and how you can get the most out of it by trading and trading. When it comes to making an investment, there are a lot of things to consider, and this book wants to get into details about every aspect needed to take conscious and smart decisions.

For all those who are looking for a complete guide on how to trade today, I wanted to create this book to find all the information useful for their investment and to avoid a possible scam! Below, I will analyze the possibility of trading today safely.

There are plenty of books on this subject on the market, thanks again for choosing this one! Every effort was made to ensure it is full of as much useful information as possible, please enjoy!

Did you know that a large percent of people who make a lot of money lose it within the first couple years?

It doesn't take much for a person to lose all of their money. Around 2 in 3 lottery winners lose all of their winnings within 5 years. If someone could lose hundreds of millions of dollars over a couple years, how fast will you lose your millions that you could make from this book?

Over the past couple years I have stumbled upon the key secret behind managing money and KEEPING it. If you follow the link below you will uncover the truth behind managing and keeping the money you make

>>> Click/Tap here to Learn the Secret Behind Money Management <<<

Or Go to https://secretstomoneymanagement.gr8.com/

Chapter 1
Basics for Beginners

This book will be a reference point for all traders, especially for all those who want to trade today but do not know where to start. This is, therefore, a guide mainly for beginners but not only where only the main topics will be addressed. In particular, it will take care from the beginning, to develop a complete guide dedicated to the basics of trading and to learn how and where to trade today.

Today, we live in the age of information technology and digitization, and this can only encourage investment. For this reason, today more than ever, that knowledge is all that is needed to trade simply and safely.

For all those who are looking for a quick and detailed way to trade today, we must not ignore it. Today, thanks to the evolution of new technologies, it is possible to trade directly from home, with online trading or directly on the stock exchange. Thanks to the Internet, new forms of investment were born, increasingly accessible and fast. Today, it is also possible to trade thanks to social trading.

Caution

Trading from home quickly and easily today does not presuppose the fact that it is easy. One should not fall into the temptation to believe that obtaining success in the practice of trading is easy and above all is exempt from risks.

Despite the evolution, the possibility of more information and more training on how and where to trade today does not presuppose the guaranteed success, but the possibility of success or failure has always remained more or less the same. It all depends on you, your training, and your dedication to trading.

How to Trade Today?

Between yesterday and today, what has changed is the way to trade money, which is the possibility for a beginner to access the necessary resources much more easily and better understand what to trade in today.

Here is the reason for this book, supported by practical examples and regulated and authorized brokers. You will find a series of useful information to better understand how and where to trade today, a step-by-step guide that will explain how and why trade in one industry today rather than another.

Starting to trade today is easy, simple, and fast! Doing it in the right way instead is a bit more difficult, especially if you do not have the right knowledge.

Where to Trade Today?

How many of you have asked yourselves this question and how many of you right now are asking? Understanding where to trade today is the technique for success! In fact, knowing where and how to trade implies a saving of time and a greater income for you traders, who will leave already in advance of the other traders, and this will lead you to become an advanced and successful trader.

In this guide, we will show you which market is the most accessible to all, the Forex, which will allow you to trade even with little savings. We will also show you what is Social Trading, which is a new form of investment based on Forex, and the sharing of information and trading strategies that will allow you to trade and become an expert in this market.

Chapter 2
Let's Talk About Capital

How Much to Trade Today?

Another fundamental point before starting to trade is understanding how much you are willing to trade today. The amount of capital that you are willing to trade changes according to the trader's economic resources but also to the degree of preparation.

For this reason, we consider it useful to advise you to start trading with a demo account, or a free trading account, which allows you to understand what are the risks of online trading but, above all, to feel the trading strategies or even just doing knowledge with the trading platform.

Given this, let's examine how much to trade today.

Trading capital today requires the following:

- The possibility of making use of its capital
- Use financial resources in fruit-bearing operations

How Much is the Capital Needed to Start Trading Today?

Many traders associate the meaning of a large sum of money to the term "capital." Obviously, there is not an equal capital for everyone, but every trader decides to trade his capital, according to what are the possibilities. So, for a basic level trader, trading €100 is equivalent to an experienced trader trading €1000.

Capital, therefore, is a relative amount for each of us. Almost always, however, capital, in its most general meaning, takes the form of a value that is very difficult to obtain and use for a possible investment. Today, we can tell you exactly what the world of online trading has become accessible to everyone, even to traders who do not have immense amounts of capital.

How Much to Trade for Tangible Results?

There are brokers that offer the possibility of trading in the stock market even with only €100 of initial capital, which is a ridiculous amount, that allows you not only to experience the world of online investment but also to get rid of wrong beliefs that online trading or stock exchange investment is only for those who own money. This is called a "test capital."

To understand this concept, we consider it to be of fundamental importance; if one understands it, the very concept of capital takes on a different meaning; in fact, it will mean every meaning of greatness or importance. In other words, the concept of capital will mean only the amount of money that is available and in the case of wrong investment does not affect the economic situation of the trader.

Be careful not to confuse this concept with the wrong concept of trading money in the wrong way. In reverse, you will have to treat the money you will trade with the utmost respect, giving it the utmost importance. Just constantly remind yourself that you earned that money by working hard; you do not want to waste it.

Remember that trading in online trading is risky and undermines the loss of the entire capital. So, pay close attention to this concept. It does not matter what the amount to trade or what capital is available. The important is to understand the value of the capital you trade.

If you follow this advice, you can find out how easy and quick to do online trading or trade in the stock market in a few steps and, especially like all of this today, how it is really affordable for everyone, thanks to the Internet. There is nothing left but to continue this path and make yours the information in this guide on how to trade today. When it comes to investment strategies, the amount invested cannot be ignored.

This chapter is oriented to the management of assets between 10,000 and one million Euros. Another premise for reading is to have a clear idea of what is meant by the amount investable.

We will divide our field of action into three bands. All three bands will assume that it has already been done:

1. Invest the maximum tax-deductible share in the supplementary pension
2. Stipulate any life insurance, which indicates that all the negative points described in the Life Insurance should be considered
3. Deduct from the investable portion any allowances for false investments, i.e., secondary activities that are genuine alternative works

The last point is particularly important for investments in real estate and land. As we will see in the operational plans, for assets up to €250,000, a speech on property and land can only be marginal.

The main reasons for the previous statement are the following:

1. Such investments often tend not to be real.

In the modern sense, an investment is such if it requires a minimum allocation of resources (for example, I buy 10,000 Euros of government bonds); otherwise, it is configured as a real activity.

Buying a home that you can then rent is the simplest example. If we interact directly with the tenant, we are doing a real activity, an alternative to our work, in which we often do not take into account the management costs and the time we spend; different is the case in which we limit ourselves to buying the house and entrust to a paid external structure the role of administrator of the building. In this second case, what remains is the real gain of the rent. The same applies when buying agricultural land; only by considering it an activity (i.e., cultivating it and managing it with appropriate decisions) will we make the most of it.

2. These investments minimize management costs only for large capital.

In fact, the realized capital gains are gross of the taxes and of all the management expenses that serve to maintain the asset in question over the years. For small investments (for example, a house worth 300,000 Euros)—inflation, taxes, maintenance costs, etc.—they reduce the real gain considerably.

Investment Instruments

As investment tools, consider the following:
1. Properties and land
2. Instruments for maximum liquidity (i.e., liquidable in up to three months)
3. Bonds
4. Stocks

The individual instruments must then be optimized following the instructions given in the following paragraphs.

We must warn against investing in alternative and typically speculative fields (art, jewelry, etc.) without having a specific capacity. These fields are, in fact, similar to alternative work: buying a painting, a prestigious watch, or a classic car; hoping for a great revaluation is completely optimistic if you are not an expert in the sector. On the other hand, if one is, it makes no sense to make it all occasional, but it would make sense to make it at least a second activity.

The proposed management is mainly passive; in the sense that we must follow the trend of our investments not continuously over time but with periodic checks (for example, quarterly) to verify whether it is appropriate to positively disinvest. For example, if a bond was bought a year ago at 95.25 and is now worth 99, a 4% gain justifies the sale; if, on the contrary, it has fallen to 94.20, it will put the heart in peace and will be held until its expiration.

From 10,000 to 50,000 Euros

We all know that it is disappointing by those who thought of diversifying, but with such a modest sum, you can only use two tools: those for maximum liquidity and bonds. You can use together or, better, use the latter unless the former is no longer advantageous due to a particular economic situation.

From 50,000 to 250,000 Euros

Here, the four instruments are all usable, obviously with due consideration.

For buildings and land, it is advisable to include them in the additional quota. If you decide to invest 50,000 Euros in real estate, instead of buying a tiny studio, it makes more sense to buy a bigger house of ownership; the fees on the added quota are less than on a second home, and there would not be all the hassles of managing an asset that, due to its small size, would yield modest yields in any case of a certain management commitment.

Also, in this case, the bonds take the largest share of the investable amount (at least 50%) and can be replaced by the instruments for maximum liquidity only in exceptional cases in which they make more.

The actions deserve separate speech. In theory, with a capital of €250,000, it would be possible to invest in the shareholder, but in practice, it is better to do so by linking the figure to one's age.

If at 30 years, an invested share of 40% can be significant; at the age of 60, it should not exceed 10%; with these data, it is automatic to remember that at the age of 40, a maximum of 30% is invested, and at most 20%, a maximum of 20%. We propose you the rule of 70: the sum between age and shareholding always makes 70.

Let us remember, however, that investing in the stock is an opportunity, not an obligation.

From 250,000 to One Million Euros

We are now in important figures. Before going into detail, it is necessary to understand "what wind it pulls." Currently, with an economy still in partial crisis, it seems that the situation is this:

secure bonds and liquidity: ****

actions: **

gold: **

properties: *

This picture will appear disappointing to those who dream of speculating with their capital, but it is certainly the one that protects it most.

With regard to property and land, up to 30% of assets can be invested in them, both as an additional share and as an investment in its own right. Many would come to invest up to 100%, but it is a too simplistic solution because, in fact, with such capital, if you want to invest in the brick, it makes more sense to undertake a real second activity. Furthermore, it should be remembered that *a property has value only if you can resell it!*

What in recent years has not been so easy and has produced losses of even 50%, just to fall from the investment made with a little liquidity.

In other words, instead of investing in a couple of luxury apartments in the city center, it is more logical to invest in smaller units by diversifying the risks that are always present on the individual investment. In any case, the crisis in the real estate sector that began in 2008 has, in fact, extinguished optimism that lasted for decades, optimism without a real rational motivation.

Once the portion allocated to property and land has been determined, the amount to be invested in shares must be determined; also, in this case, the maximum is represented by the rule of 70. The remaining part is destined to the bonds.

Let's See Some "Sensible" Cases.

James, 37,—investable amount €350,000—decides to have an additional share of 100,000 Euros to his house and invests 20% in shares (70,000 Euros) and the remainder in bonds (180,000).

Sara, 45,—investor 450,000—decides not to have an additional quota, buys a 110,000 euro housing unit that rents, invests 10% in shares (45,000 Euros), 260,000 Euros in bonds, and 35,000 Euros in an online account now particularly cheap.

Patrick, 42,—investable amount 700,000—decides to have a house a little bigger for his family (additional share of 100,000 Euros) and invests a 25% in shares (175,000) and the rest all in bonds, well 425,000 Euros.

Donald, 60,—investable amount €1,000,000—The house does not change it; not particularly trusting in real estate investing, it invests 100,000 Euros in shares, 100,000 in an online account, 50,000 in a normal bank account, and a good 750,000 Euros in bonds, suitably diversified.

Chapter 3
How to Use Money

Understanding that investment must earn money for those who trade them is a fundamental concept. Although it may seem rather trivial, not no is and above all not all are of the same idea. Understanding which sectors to bet on is not trivial!

There are two possible ways to trade money. Trading money also means making money work for you. Here is, therefore, explained the reason for why trading money.

In fact, we know that money is one of the major components of the budget of every single man. Money serves and is the basis of a myriad of fundamental activities that belong to our lives.

The two roads to follow are divided between:

1. Have the money
2. Use the money

To better explain these concepts, let's make a trivial example.

It is commonplace to say: Put the savings under the mattress. This concept, although quite trivial, makes us understand how this method makes us owners of money.

However, owning money does not require any investment. For them to yield, they must be traded. The money must, therefore, be used, or traded, not just hold. This is especially true when considering the constant loss of value cash undergoes every year due to inflation. Trading can be seen as a way to betting against money itself, and this is what I tend to think about when considering an opportunity.

How to Use the Capital to Trade?

It is possible to use the money to go shopping, to buy consumer goods, such as a new smartphone, a new car, or even other consumer goods.

Even having a small amount of money deposited in the bank or other investment funds, however, is not a wrong solution. In all these cases, money is traded and yields. Here is the concept that explains how to use the money to make more money. This is precisely the concept of trading today.

If you use the money to trade in investment funds, it is sure that they are used to make money. In this case, producing money does not require much effort and no new initiative on your part. We only have to hope that the markets we have invested in are always positive, that is, they always close with a gain for us. Of course, it does not mean that you can forget and forget about it, but you will always be the ones to decide how and where to trade them.

To do this, you rely on financial magnates or choose to trade in online trading or other markets, thanks to online brokers, who offer you a complete training on the markets and online trading, which will then allow you to trade your money and make your capital the right choices based on those that are your strategies.

Thanks to the training courses, you will be aware of some theoretical and technical factors. The more information you have, the greater the chances of earning for you.

Trading Money Today: Two Ways to Trade Money

We can divide the investment into the two big categories:

1. Buy a good, wait for its value to increase, and then resell it at a higher value so that you can even make a profit. In this case, most traders buy and sell real estate.
2. Trading by buying shares. In this case, the trader becomes the owner of a piece of the company for which he has taken out an action, with the hope that the value of the stock will rise so that he can then sell his stock to a new buyer or shareholder and collect the profit.

At the moment, the focus will be more on this last aspect, as we consider the most developed and certainly will be the one that allows greater diversification of the portfolio.

Trading in the stock market today is also possible, thanks to options trading. In this case, thanks to the options trading, it is possible to trade in shares and also earn downwards. Buying a financial instrument of this type, therefore, allows you to earn even if the value of this goes down.

Another widely used strategy to trade today and to capitalize on its capital is to lend money for a certain period of time and then receive it with interest. Today, we talk a lot about this sector and especially about bond investment.

Investing in Bonds

When we talk about bond investment, we are certainly talking about investment in Italian bots, or English bonds, or German bunds.

Purchasing an American bot means lending to the state your money for the value of the bot at that time. The state will subsequently undertake to return them on a specific date, with the addition of pre-established interests, without the possibility of escaping this payment.

Another example is the purchase of bonds. In this way, you lend your money to the company that issued the bonds. It is not just a matter of state bodies, but also of private bodies. In this sense, the company will compensate us after a certain period by paying us an interest in the form of coupons.

These are currently the easiest ways to trade today, of alternative methods to commit your money, and make money with them. In the following chapter, we will also continue to talk about sectors in which to trade today, each category, with its own merits and defects.

Chapter 4
What Trading is NOT

Once you understand what it means to trade today, your money, it is of fundamental importance, even understand what is not an investment! Above all, understand how you must trade your money but also understand what an investment IS NOT. This last concept is not familiar to everyone; in fact, in most cases, they do not even recognize it.

Please note that trading in online trading is not the same as gambling. It is a form of pure investment, which involves its risks but which must not be compared to gambling.

You do not choose to trade in a company as I would choose a number at the casino roulette. To trade, you need to know the trend of the market and what it entails.

Unfortunately, many traders still make this mess. So, here is the wrong term to play on the stock exchange rather than trade in the stock market. This difference is not unimportant.

The art of trading is essentially based on reasonable expectations, which derive mainly from statistics or from professional studies done in that sector.

An investment is based on essential components:

1. Study
2. Experience
3. Certain facts

Obviously, the risk when trading always exists but cannot be compared to gambling. There are statistics as there are systems that work thanks to the fact that they are able to produce a profit in the best possible way and in the shortest possible time.

Therefore, the trader will have to learn to know and to favor those investment systems that statistically, in the long run, are winners. Never forget the risk associated with online trading. Only by accepting and living with the risk can we trade seriously and in a balanced way. It is, therefore, knowing the risk that it can be controlled and managed.

Tools for Financial Investment

Given the above, we will go into more specific, to learn more about what are safe investment today. Many also ask what are the main methods of common investment for a person of medium and low level, with a modest budget if not limited, and especially if it exists, something simple to start with, perhaps in a very short time?

With all frankness, that there is nothing difficult but only a complex that does not mean you cannot do it! The world of finance is constantly evolving; the classical methods of investment, even if they have not waned, have been greatly reduced and have given way to these new forms of investment.

Knowing most of it is one of the first rules for a good investment. The first rule to diversify risk is by diversifying the portfolio or trading in different types of assets.

Trading Shares as an Investment Tool

A title representing a share of a company's property is called stock. Owning one or more shares of a public limited company also implies the possibility of earning with it, as a member of that company. In this case, we speak of being a shareholder and expressing one's right to vote, having the right to earn from the profits produced by that company, to an extent that is proportional to the number of shares held.

Trading Shares

For example, if you own 1% in a company's shares, you can collect 1% when the company decides to distribute the so-called dividends.

Pay attention, however, to the fact that not all companies are equal, and there is also a diversification regarding the payment of dividends to its shareholders. In that case, those holding their own shares will be able to capitalize on their investment by earning the increase in value of their shares or even by the subsequent sale of these shares to another trader.

The stocks of this company must, however, be subject to fundamental laws of the market, related to supply and demand, but above all, we must remember that the more a society is strong, the stronger its action will be; as a result, their value will tend to grow. In the opposite case, on the other hand, in the case in which the weakness of the company will be greater, the less will be the attraction for those actions.

In short, this means that if an action does not pay dividends, it is possible that gains are obtained with the increase in value of these, by retrading or speculating on the differential between the selling price and the purchase price. The percentages of return in this case on the investment are very high, but there is also the fact that there are many risks, as well as the possibility that this does not go up in value, or worse, that it loses.

Trading Bonds

If, instead, you decide to trade in bonds, as we mentioned earlier, it means trading in debt securities. These securities are issued by companies or public bodies, which allow the holder to have the right to obtain a repayment of the principal lent to the issuer at maturity, plus an interest in this sum.

Possession of Italian bonds or btp, or English bonds, means, having lent money to a company or even to a state and then have in hand, a title that certifies the debt owed to you and that will then have to pay by a specific date. This, therefore, also presupposes a payment of a preestablished interest to honor the aforementioned loan.

In most cases, the greater the risk of the insolvency company, the greater the interest will be. In the opposite case, the lower the risk, the lower the interest will be.

But there is also another case where interests may be greater. In this case, not necessarily the company must be insolvent, but it may also happen that this is less tempting than others, and in this case, the customer will put into circulation bonds that pay a greater interest.

The most famous bonds I mention are the following:

- Italian government bonds, BOTs or BTPs
- German bonds
- American or English bonds

Trading Common Funds

Those who instead opt for trading in sound investment mutual funds that can use financial instruments that are also defined as shares of investment funds and that collect the money of savers who entrust the management of their savings to the companies of management, which have legal personality and capital different from those of the fund.

In short, when you trade in a fund, you choose to become part of a group of people, who have collected their money together. These, in turn, deliver their money to an experienced trader to get it managed.

The manager's arduous task will be to understand, with which capital he has been given, which shares and bonds to buy; in this way, the mutual fund will be built. Based on your stake in that fund, earnings will be distributed.

At the moment, there are different types of funds. In this sense, we can distinguish the following:

1. Funds that trade on baskets of securities
2. Funds that tend to replicate indices or a set of indices

3. Passively managed funds
4. Actively managed funds as well as hedge funds.

In most cases, the funds are linked to provisioning plans or insurance policies that are subscribed by users, who are not willing to spend their time to understand how and where to trade.

Advantages and Disadvantages of Mutual Funds

At the moment, there are many advantages linked to mutual funds but also many disadvantages. Among the main disadvantages, there is the fact that the returns related to the investment are often mediocre, penalized in many cases also by the high running costs. The manager must be paid, even if no profits are obtained. For this reason, management risks are always lurking. As Anthony Robbins once stated, 96% of mutual funds do not beat or draw the market in 10 years.

On the opposite side, however, there are several advantages, especially for those who have a large investment capacity. In this case, those who use the mutual funds, use them to keep the capital protected from inflation and also why not, to earn something. In much more elementary terms, inflation means higher prices for goods and services. This means a reduction of purchasing power.

In short, if today with the assets set aside you can buy a certain number of goods and services, does not mean that in a few years with the same money, you can buy them anyway. This for the simple reason that the price of those goods and services will be increased due to inflation. In technical terms, this also means a decrease in purchasing power.

Speculative Investment Instruments

Until now, I have seen three categories of investment that include the actual purchase of an asset, regardless of whether it is an action, a security, or a share, which must be held and held pending generate returns due precisely to appreciation.

Below, however, is a list of a series of tools that do not provide for the purchase of an asset, but above all, it is not necessarily due to things that the asset should be appreciated to generate a profit. In this case, we are talking about speculative investment and short selling. These presuppose the possibility of earning also following the depreciation of a particular asset.

In most cases, traders and investors talk about these investments, as well as investment in derivatives. This is because their price derives from the market value of another financial instrument, which is defined as underlying. For example, the underlying market is defined as investment in stocks, financial indices, currencies, interest rates, etc.

Trading Options

According to the technical jargon, the option is defined as a contract that gives the holder the right, but not the obligation to buy or sell the security on which the option is written. Obviously, everything has at a certain exercise price and by a certain date.

In short, with an option contract, you have the right but not the obligation to buy or sell an asset at a certain price and within a certain date, making the payment of the cost immediately to obtain this right. If conditions are favorable to the trader, this can confirm the purchase or sale, according to the option reported, yielding the investment.

In the opposite case, however, if the conditions are not favorable to the trader, no operation will be concluded, but the loss will be avoided, even if the initial cost paid has not been recovered. Within this basic operation, there are also several advanced strategies, such as that of selling these contracts instead of buying them.

Trading Futures

When we talk about futures contracts, this refers to a type of futures contract. In this contract, the parties undertake to exchange, on a given date, a certain quantity of certain financial assets at the set price.

In practice, when working with futures contracts, the trader obtains the right to buy or sell an asset at the price and on a fixed date, as soon as the transaction is opened. When the futures contract is resolved, the trader will be able to benefit from it and obtain an income, due to the difference between the purchase price or the selling price established with the future, and the current market price of the asset underlying the future itself.

As in everything, if the difference is positive, a profit will be realized; otherwise, a loss will occur. When we talk about futures contracts, we always refer to underlying assets of the futures. These are divided into categories:

1. *Real categories.* Such as commodities, i.e., raw materials such as wheat, gold, metals, coffee, etc.

2. *Financial categories.* Only in this case will we talk about financial futures, whose underlying assets may be, for example, a currency, currency futures, or a stock exchange index.

Trading Forex

The Forex market, which stands for Foreign Exchange Market, is the currency market, which is the largest market in the world, if not the best known in our time. Forex is not only defined as an investment tool but a real market, where it is possible to trade through different instruments, such as options or futures or, even simply, buy and sell, thanks to the spot market.

In the Forex market, only currency pairs are exchanged, and there are no other assets. Consequently, the currency that you buy or sell, you do not buy it or sell it individually, but always in pairs. Therefore, all traders and speculators trade precisely in the fact of this change, or trade on the exchange, on the fact that a currency grows and one decreases.

To make Forex trading, if, on the one hand, presupposes the possibility of bringing home a positive result, on the other hand, it assumes the risk of complete insolvency or, in other words, the total loss of capital traded.

Furthermore, trading in the Forex market also requires a fairly complete level of knowledge and experience. That's why we always recommend only regulated brokers, which, in addition to ensuring the capital of the trader, also manages to ensure adequate training of the trader.

Chapter 5
Social Trading

Social Trading can be defined as one of the best strategies, in our opinion, of online trading. Thanks to social trading, traders can share their strategies with each other, but they can also ask for advice on the type of investment.

It is not recently that we talk about social trading and copy trader, just in online trading. One of the best brokers to offer this service is eToro, a veteran and the founding father of social trading and copy trader, which allows all traders to trade by copying the best traders.

Thanks to Social Trading, the trader is the direct manager of their own money, that is, he does not entrust them to any external manager, as with the online trading platforms, he will be the owner of his own capital and will be responsible for his own investment.

At the same time, however, it is not the trader who has to buy or sell, but thanks to specialized trading platforms, the trader can view a portfolio of market participants called traders, observe them, and compare and share their strategies and style and the trader's performance. In case they are interested in this trader, they can also decide to link to his account to the chosen trader, thanks to the copy trader system.

When you copy your chosen trader, all transactions made by that trader will be photocopied directly on his personal account; in short, it will be automatically replicated on the trader's account through the Social Trading platform.

So, it will not be the trader to carry out the trading operations, but the trader that has been decided to copy that will work for us. Obviously, this will earn a percentage of our earnings, while those who trade will earn the percentage traded on that trade.

Stock Trading

To operate with social trading, you just have to open an online trading account with eToro, choose your favorite traders, and bet on them. These will generate profits on our behalf. The trader is only responsible for diversifying the portfolio and choosing the best traders to follow.

The gains that can be obtained obviously change from trader to trader but, above all, on the basis of traded capital, as well as losses. In our opinion, we can only say that the profit percentages, for each positive trade, are higher than those of bonds and shares, as well as investment times can be shortened.

The risk associated with online trading certainly exists but, if you take the due precautions, thanks to the right knowledge, certainly can be reduced, even compared to the Forex DIY, seen and considered that the trader copied, is not a beginner trader but an expert, also confirmed by the profits he has earned.

Chapter 6
Trading and Time

When one thinks of the different investment tools, if not the practice, of the investment in general, one cannot but considers the temporal factor. This is one of the factors that other miller discourages the trader. But why?

In these times, we are so used to the concept of *everything and immediately* we cannot wait any longer. We demand everything immediately, also losing track of time and the precious value of time.

Unfortunately, in online trading, you cannot expect to have everything and immediately, but above all, we cannot expect to become experienced traders and professionals in just under a month or worse than a week.

You cannot think of becoming an expert trader if you do not want to study and practice! In online trading, but also in investment, in general, it takes time to learn how to trade. Another advice that is not feasible at the moment is to think about spending some time to find a deserving, professional, and worthy investment and investment technique.

When trading, it must be done seriously and professionally. If, for example, we trade in a trading strategy based on currency trading, with a maximum payout of 65% for a positively closed trade, then we must enter the perspective that we must give money to work with a specific strategy.

If you are following the market trend, it will be counterproductive to exit the market because, in addition to losing its capital, you may not even get the desired return. That's why time is money, and it should not be wasted unnecessarily. Above all, hurry is a bad companion.

The time factor is also one of the main factors for which it is decided better to entrust its capital to a financial expert so that this is to make the choices for them. Very often, however, this trust is not always repaid by an increase in one's capital. Most often this capital is completely lost.

The Importance of the Right Time and Timing

Understanding when the right time to trade is very important. Giving money to mature is certainly one of the most determining factors for the success of your investment. The fundamental concept remains the same: within what you want to earn money and how to earn them.

To make sure that you know, in advance, how much you can earn and how to make money for us, you cannot rely on chance, and above all, we cannot expect to waste time but not even to demand everything immediately.

Everything has its time; also in investment, they have their right times and their importance. As you can see, even the right timing serves to give way to the investment, to make your own cycle, and to express that reasonable expectation. The right setup also serves your capital to survive in any situation, resist negative moments, and always have the strength to start again.

Avoiding Risks

To better understand the risks involved in trading in risky strategies, it seems right to remember those that are the right principles. Suppose you can trade $10,000 in a strategy that is 50% risk. This strategy was put in place to double the capital within a maximum of 3. Highly risky strategy from our point of view as it could result in the total loss of the entire capital. This operation is recommended only to experienced traders.

With this example, we have made you understand how these operations allow you to double or triple the capital within a few months but also how you can lose all your capital in a matter of months. In fact, by implementing these dangerous strategies, you will also see the account halved, or entirely burned, within a few weeks.

To understand everything better, let's take another example. According to your trading strategies, you have traded on a particular asset with a strategy and think that this can give you a return of 50% within a month.

To not fall into error, we advise you to set the opposite goal or try to ask the question: how would it be if in half a month you lost half of the bill? Here is therefore explained and understood in a simple and fast way on what is the right time, but especially those that are the wrong strategies not to be adopted.

Limiting Damages of Social Trading

Many wonder if social trading is the right strategy to avoid wasting time and earning, thanks to social trading. Before proceeding, we remind you that social trading is not a risk-free form of trading, even if the risk, in this case, is reduced. To trade in social trading, we believe it is essential to operate for a period of time between 9 and 12 months minimum. This is for one simple reason. Before choosing an investment system, you must see the performance for at least a year. In this sense, there is no need to follow a trader, 24 hours a day, 365 days a year, but only that you have to consult all the data of all the operations performed during the year, perhaps with the help with special tools that simplify reading.

Once you understand how to trade, but above all, you understand how much trading and who you want to trade in, you have to consider the risk that you are willing to run. Beyond this limit, it is advisable to leave it alone.

In most cases, the conditions that have led you to make a certain investment choice must have solid foundations so that the investment can yield. That's why a period of 12 months is a period enough to make you understand if your investment is right or wrong.

Chapter 7
Trading and Commitment

Time is a tyrant, but not always! The first thing you have to concentrate on to put in place a good investment is the time you want to dedicate to the investment itself, or even to learn the new discipline with which you want to operate.

Our advice is to take all the time necessary to study the new techniques, to implement the new strategies, and to metabolize all the concepts well. Only after you have done this, we advise you to start trading in the stock market or trading with an online demo account.

Even if your investment objective is different from online trading, there's no problem. The important thing is to continue and persist in your own way to achieve the precise objective.

Have a Clear Goal

Another point on which we will focus is the investment objective. This point is very important for the trader and for his success also based on what is the psychology of an individual.

However, knowing how to do it is not a foregone conclusion. This presupposes a good capacity for analysis. In fact, in the investment, there is only the objective to be achieved; there is nothing but the possibility of victory and the possibility of losses and risks.

1) **Be the owner of your own money.**

Being owners of their own money presupposes the possibility of being aware of recognizing one's own limits, having a precise objective and above all having the theoretical foundations to achieve it. In this sense, we must put ourselves in the advantageous condition of knowing which risks we can run. Recognizing them is really the starting point for a good investment. It would not make sense to start a new investment if you do not know the limits and do not know what the risks related to it are.

2) **Know yourself.**

Once the first point has been made, and the objective is clear but also the risk related to the loss of one's own money, one has to do is start analyzing oneself. In this way, we can understand whether it is worthwhile trading with long-term strategies or short-term strategies, whether it is better to trade a certain capital rather than another, or better diversify investment objectives. It is better not to make fun of yourself if you do not want to lose your capital completely, you must recognize your limits, predict any reactions, and risk tolerance levels.

To better understand, let's take a practical example. Suppose we have two investment strategies. In both cases, the aim is to achieve 50% increase in initial capital. Based on what is in the first statistic, you can get a profit of 50% over a year, risking half the capital. According to the second strategy, on the other hand, we will obtain a profit of 50% over 2 years, but in a maximum period of 24 months, risking only 20% of the capital. At this point, a question arises: what kind of strategy to use? In the first case, it is true that the goal is reached first, but it is also true that the percentages in case of loss are greater. If you come to check a negative period of time, even just three months, it is not easy not to consider it as a problem. Without making fun of it, nobody likes losing, and losing half of their capital can be a real blow to everyone.

But there is also the positive side; after the black period of three months, one could follow with half of the remaining capital and could concentrate on the remaining months to complete its strategy and make a profit. Once the negative moment has passed, the strategy begins to grind very good operations, and in the following 9 months, the account recovers not only the losses but closes positively with a further increase. Now, this we have proposed to you is just one example. Not all traders close their accounts in a year. So, pay close attention. In the second case, however, the strategy can be used by all those who prefer to operate more safely and that we recommend because it limits the risk even if the waiting time is greater.

3) **Objective = Earnings; Objective = Risk**

Another important point to keep in mind and that must always be considered is what you want to earn, but above all, we are willing to risk to get that profit. Many times, it is more useful to rely on instinct and not on rationality, but this method does not always work. In this sense, we want to understand that it is much more prudent to evaluate the situation in which we find ourselves from time to time, to prefix the objectives we want to achieve at a given moment, and the possibility we have of reaching that goal. Therefore, knowing oneself before starting an investment is an excellent strategy to understand even the real goals and the real risks we can bear.

Chapter 8
Compound Interest

Compound interest is one of the most powerful tools at your disposal, so study it carefully. It is an interest that is not collected but is added to the initial capital that generated it to be traded again.

This means that for the period following the one that generated the interest, interests will be traded and accrued not only on the initial capital but also on the interest accrued in the first period.

In a subsequent period, the discussion does not change; the interest will always accrue on the initial capital, to whose capital are added also the interest accrued in the first period and the interest accrued in the second period (which, in turn, have accrued on the interests of the former).

How to Calculate Compound Interests

Suppose you have the opportunity to trade with an initial capital of $10,000. In this case, you will choose an investment plan that can guarantee a minimum return of 10% per annum for 5 years. During the first year, you decide to take the accrued interest out of the investment.

At this point, after the first 5 years of investment, you will have collected $1000 per year for 5 years which, together with the initial capital, make a total of $15,000. If, on the other hand, it is decided to trade the interests again, exploiting the compound interest system, you will have, at the end of the 5 years, the total capital of $16,105.10.

If the entire capital is redeemed again for another 5 years, you will have a total capital of $20,000, using the first strategy, while reinvesting the interest could also reach the figure of $25,937.42.

Trade Today With Compound Interests

Compound interests need a long enough time to function better. In fact, time is a fundamental factor for them. Patience and just time are two very important factors to allow the interests to mature significantly on themselves. We can also consider trading on compound interest with social trading. The investment process will be the same, for most transactions, based on what is the investment capital.

Assuming we obtain a monthly return of 5%, we also decide to trade the interests, trading and increasing in this way the weight of the transactions that will be replicated. So, based on what has been stated so far, we can tell you that time works for you and that the more you learn how to use it, the more it pays off.

Now, the first thing to do is to understand that compounded interests are also a form of investment and that compound interests are an excellent tool for increasing capital.

If you think, then, that if you have a modest capital or you have a capital to trade, and you hope to get exaggerated interests, then you really are completely out of the way.

Chapter 9
Investing in Yourself

As I have already said and repeatedly stated, trading does not mean betting, let alone gambling. Trading means being based on precise studies and statistics. This is the only method that allows you to find reasonable expectations of success to also exploit a specific strategy.

The greater your studies will be, the more strategies will be learned, the lower the chances of running into mistakes, the greater the returns will be, and the lower the risks of losing one's capital.

The greater the time to devote to study and to learning, the greater the successes that can be achieved. However, there is also the risk of studying and applying a lot. The risk cannot be canceled; at most, it can be reduced.

Unfortunately, all investments are based essentially on people and their decisions. There is no investment for everyone, and there is no equal strategy for everyone. There are many strategies for many traders, not mathematical laws.

Fear and greed are the two emotions that must be controlled if you want to succeed in the right investment. Both these emotions move the markets. Although they are two human conditions that can be studied and analyzed, they can never be translated into perfect mathematical laws.

Even if you trade with a strategy that allows you to close in profit more than 90% of the time, 10% represents the risk and must not be put aside but must always be considered. This happens very often to traders or investors who do not want to close the operations at a loss or do not want to abandon the wrong investment admitting the mistake because they believe that sooner or later they will return in their favor.

Chapter 10
Should You Challenge the Market?

One of the fundamental strategies for not losing the entire capital is to consider the risk related to market movements but, above all, to never challenge the market and go against the trend.

Trading in the stock market is not easy; even the strategy of the best traders can turn out to be a failure if you insist on challenging the market. Never think about this but, above all, never consider a movement of the market equal to the other. So, you never have to think about being able to beat the market ahead of time.

It is advisable not to challenge the market but, above all, to keep in mind that the market is always right. If you want to trade in serious and professional ways, you have to study, set a strategy, and follow it both positively and negatively if the initial conditions are always the same.

In the case instead of changing the starting conditions, we suggest to evaluate everything with a cold mind and evaluate whether it is still appropriate to continue on that road or change the road. This means accepting the error, but it is always better to understand the mistake of losing the entire capital.

Chapter 11
Portfolios and Diversification

The best money protection strategy is portfolio diversification. The investment portfolio is certainly one of the terms the traders feel most when it comes to investment. But what is the portfolio?

The investment portfolio can be understood as a combination of suitably combined financial assets to achieve the objective. In other words, it represents the set of all financial products or strategies on which you have decided to trade.

Advantages of the Diversified Portfolio

So, diversifying your portfolio is crucial to gain and suffer the effects of losses as little as possible. In fact, the goal of the trader is to earn in the long term and not in the short term.

Therefore, the best strategy is to diversify the portfolio and to unite different types of instruments that operate in different ways to reduce the overall risk of the investment itself. We can also consider that investments, with a diversification of the portfolio, are statistically less than a little or no diversified at all.

If the trader decides to trade in stocks and bonds by diversifying his portfolio, then we can consider different hypotheses. We can, therefore, consider bonds as safer instruments than stocks. In this case, the trader who wants a conservative portfolio, or trading with a low risk, we recommend trading two-thirds of his capital per bond, while a small part allocates it to the shares. If, on the other hand, you prefer a more aggressive approach, or a higher profit, based on the level of risk you are willing to run, then it is preferable to trade at least two-thirds of your capital to the shares and the remainder to bonds and funds.

Trading With Government Bonds: Right or Wrong?

For those who want to trade in bonds, or even for those who want to trade in much safer sectors, even if less profitable, we recommend government bonds. Taking into consideration the government bonds, we can see how these are divided into different categories based on what is the degree of security and return.

To trade with government bonds, the rating agencies are used as Standard & Poor's, Moody's and Fitch, and the Rate, i.e., the votes, AAA, AA +, etc. By diversifying the portfolio with government bonds, it will be possible to trade two-thirds in bonds or 65% in government bonds or sovereign national institutions, but which have a rating of AAA or AA +, while the remainder allocates it to instruments bonds with lower rating ratings and more remunerative coupon rates.

The same strategy could be used for stocks. Using a more conservative approach, you can choose solid company shares that generate income over the long term. Trading the entire capital on a single Signal Provider is not the best solution, and we never recommend it. Obviously, attention is used to distinguish the parameters with which we analyze the performance of a trader, thanks to which it is possible to distinguish the conservative Signal Providers from the more aggressive ones.

Finally, we remind you never to exaggerate even in the diversification of the portfolio. Diversifying the portfolio excessively is not the right strategy, but above all, it is not suitable for beginners.

Conclusion

Thank you for making it through to the end of *Stock Trading*, let's hope it was informative and provides you with all of the tools you need to achieve your goals whatever they may be.

The next step is to start applying what you have learned during this book and get started right away. Our suggestion is always to open up a demo account and make a few tries, before putting real money into it. Remember that you should never risk more than what you can afford to lose, so manage your capital wisely and take out profits regularly.

Finally, if you found this book useful in any way, a review on Amazon is always appreciated!

Did you know that a large percent of people who make a lot of money lose it within the first couple years?

It doesn't take much for a person to lose all of their money. Around 2 in 3 lottery winners lose all of their winnings within 5 years. If someone could lose hundreds of millions of dollars over a couple years, how fast will you lose your millions that you could make from this book?

Over the past couple years I have stumbled upon the key secret behind managing money and KEEPING it. If you follow the link below you will uncover the truth behind managing and keeping the money you make

>>> Click/Tap here to Learn the Secret Behind Money Management <<<

Or Go to https://secretstomoneymanagement.gr8.com/

Description

Are you looking for a great book about trading stocks but every single time you purchase a course it seems that nothing makes sense? Are you scared when you hear words like "trendline," "bonds," and "futures"?

Then, this is the right book for you! In *Stock Trading*, you are going to learn everything there is to know about this topic and get insightful tips that will transform your mindset when it comes to money.

During this in-depth manual, you are going to learn about fundamental topics such as the following:

- What initial capital is required to start so that you know if you have the right credentials to get started in this amazing world or if it is time to save money before going on the attack
- What big boys do to stay ahead of the competition and get the best deals, making money even when stocks are falling
- What social trading is and how you can benefit from it
- What trading is not and how you can avoid the main mistakes of beginners
- How to time the market correctly and get the most out of your trades
- A lot of hidden information that will boost your education and get you started investing as fast as possible

As you can see, this book is full of details and goes very deep on the subject. Prior experience is not required, and the manual was written especially for those who do not know anything about investing.

If you have been on the fence for a while and want to take your investing game to the next level, this is the right book for you. Get it now at a special price and act fast; it won't be so cheap forever.